Benjamin Charles Steele
Japanese Identification Card

To Tom O'Connor
with Best Wishes

Ben Steele

Benjamin Charles Steele

PRISONER OF WAR

An exhibition of eighty drawings and three paintings in the Northcutt Gallery of Art in the Department of Art at Eastern Montana College, Billings, Montana, September 17 to October 16, 1986. This entire collection of artworks has been given to the college by Mr. Steele for its permanent collection.

EDITED, WITH AN INTRODUCTION by
Alan Newberg
Professor of Art
Eastern Montana College

ESSAY by
James Todd
Professor of Art and Humanities
University of Montana

CAPTIONS by
Shirley Steele with
Benjamin C. Steele
Professor of Art Emeritus
Eastern Montana College

Cover Illustration:
"The Water Line"
Oil on Hardboard, 24" by 48"

At Camp O'Donnell one water spigot serves the entire camp.
POW's who are able carry water to sick comrades who cannot
get their own. Well soldiers string canteens together on a stick
or hollow out bamboo by poking through the connecting
membranes to make water carriers. Soldiers stand in the
waterline all day and half the night, waiting their turns. Many
collapse and die before getting a drink.

Edited by Alan Newberg
Editorial Assistant: Linda Hammond
Design by Alan Newberg
Typesetting by Pre-Vue Publications, Billings, Montana
Printing by Color World Printers, Bozeman, Montana

Eastern Montana College Bookstore
1500 North Thirtieth Street
Billings, Montana 59101

Acknowledgements

This publication would not have been possible without the efforts and support of many friends and associates. Thanks to Linda Hammond for her role in nearly every phase of the writing and publication of this catalog. She accepted it as a project for a three-credit practicum course and became an invaluable assistant as a consequence. She wrote letters, taped the commentaries for the captions, developed time lines, and otherwise attended to a myriad of details. Jean Rahn also deserves special mention. In her role as director of the Eastern Montana College Foundation, she assisted and encouraged me with this project in many ways. Besides giving moral support, she was especially helpful in identifying funds that could be used for the project, even in the developmental stages. Ken Heikes in his dual roles of chief financial officer for the college and treasurer for the Foundation deserves much credit. His creative financing ideas greatly facilitated the project. Amy Gibler, manager of the Eastern Montana College Bookstore, must be thanked for underwriting a portion of the costs and for handling the sales of the catalog. The Eastern Montana College Foundation, its board and its project screening committees must also be thanked for providing additional support. Dave Servies, President of the Board, diligently attended to details of the gift of the collection to the college.

James Todd is to be commended for his provocative and authoritative essay. His twenty-year scholarly investigation of art which addresses major social ideals and conflicts of our times lends special depth to his comments. Special thanks is extended as well to Jim Healey of the Eastern Montana College Department of English for editorial proofreading of the texts. Thanks also is extended to my wife, Ellen Newberg, and to Whitney Hanson, Art Department secretary, both of whom provided additional editorial comment and insight as well as proofreading and general support. A very special thank you also goes to Shirley Steele who worked particularly diligently with me in writing the introduction and with Ben in writing the captions, correcting inaccuracies and suggesting improved phrasing.

This project also owes a great deal to Ken Woosley, Director of News Media Services on campus. He generously provided the support of his office, including Joe Heins, and staff writer Chuck Rightmire. Thank yous are also extended to Stanley Burgard of Color World Printers and Kent von Isser, photographer.

Paula Diegert, Director of the Eastern Montana College Alumni Association; Troy Dalton, Director of the Northcutt Gallery; and Fred Magers, Gallery Assistant, are all thanked for their cooperative efforts in sponsoring and curating the Prisoner of War Exhibit.

Finally, and most importantly, I thank Ben Steele for making the gift of the Prisoner of War collection to Eastern Montana College.—Alan Newberg, editor.

Introduction

By Alan Newberg
Professor of Art
Eastern Montana College

The bombing of Pearl Harbor on December 7, 1941, will always be a day of infamy for the people of the United States. However, many Americans do not realize that only ten hours later the Japanese launched an equally devastating attack on our bases in the Philippines.[1] In many respects, this action had an even greater consequence upon the course of World War II in the Pacific Theater than the bombing of Pearl Harbor. Within a few days the Japanese had invaded the Philippines. In three weeks they drove our forces into the Bataan Peninsula and, by April, 1942, had forced them to surrender. Eight thousand American and forty thousand Philippine soldiers were taken prisoner. For these men, this was the beginning of an ordeal which was to become one of the greatest horrors of the war. Immediately after their capture, the exhausted and emaciated soldiers were forced to march nearly sixty miles virtually nonstop with almost no provision for food or water. Many died. Afterwards, the survivors were held in a series of prison camps and placed on forced labor details with minimal provisions and no medicines. Hundreds more died. Many of the American prisoners were ultimately shipped to mainland Japan where they were forced to labor in coal mines, smelters, and factories.

One of the survivors of Bataan and the prison camps of the Philippines and Japan was a Montanan, Benjamin Charles Steele. He has distinguished himself among those survivors by having produced a series of eighty drawings and three paintings which depict his experiences during the three and one half years that he was a prisoner of war. These artworks comprise one of the most comprehensive and expressively powerful visual records of the prisoner-of-war experience under the Japanese. Steele's collection of prisoner-of-war art is the subject of this exhibit and catalog.

During the seventeen years that I have known Ben Steele, I have come to believe that he is an extraordinary human being. One of the best-liked people I have ever known, he is respected and loved by hundreds of students, colleagues, and people who form the broader community beyond the college campus. I have identified three major factors in Ben's life that I believe have enabled him to become the remarkable person he is—he is a native Montanan, he is an ex-prisoner of war, and he is an artist.

Today, Ben Steele is Professor of Art Emeritus at Eastern Montana College. A member of the art faculty at Eastern Montana College for twenty-two years, he served as chairman of the Art Department for more than half of that time. He was the chairman when I joined the faculty in 1969. For the past four years, he has come out of retirement each winter quarter to teach courses in painting and drawing. Just over one year ago, I asked Ben if he would consider donating his Prisoner of War Collection to the Art Department at Eastern Montana College. He said he would, and this project began.

Even as I first talked to Ben about donating his Prisoner of War Collection, I knew that what most motivated me was more than the story of the ordeals and atrocities of the war that these artworks tell so graphically. It was also the fact that Ben has become someone everyone feels enriched to know. Like Goya's etchings, "The Horrors of War," this body of eighty drawings and three paintings is a powerful condemnation of dark and inhuman things that people do to one another under the cold and tolerant eye of war. Ben's drawings warrant comparison with the great works from the history of art that protest the irrationality and immorality of war. However, it is important to speak of the social functions that art can have on an artist and his audience. I write of this aspect of the meaning

1

and content of Ben's work, an aspect which I perceive to have shaped his character and which is related to the kind of person he has become.

Ben recalls that he began to draw in Bilibid Prison while he was immobilized by illness. Although he had sketched as part of grade school classes, he does not recall any particular inclination toward art during his youth. Initially, in prison he drew to pass the hours of his convalescence and to combat boredom. At first he drew scenes and recollections of his life in Montana. However, some of the other prisoners encouraged him to draw life in the compound, so he did. It is important to note that all but two of the drawings done in the prison camps were destroyed. However, these drawings are not lost. When the war was over and the prisoners were returned to the States, they required extensive psychological and medical attention to make the adjustment back to civilian life. When the psychiatrists learned that he had taken up drawing during captivity, they encouraged Ben to draw again. Not only was he able to recall with accuracy the visual details of the ordeal, but he also was able to recreate many of the lost drawings exactly as they had originally been executed.

Meaning in art, as in life, is an elusive quality. Over the years as Ben has shared his experiences with me via bits of vividly told stories, I have marveled at his openness and even more at his lack of bitterness. Despite the grisly nature of his experiences, he seems to enjoy recalling them. I am sure that he could not have created these artworks had he not drawn them first while in the camps. If he had merely drawn them from memory after his release, they would lack the verisimilitude of feeling and authenticity of detail that these works possess. They would mean less.

Among the more telling accounts that Ben has shared with me is how, on the march, some of the soldiers gave up. When this happened, the Japanese guards prodded them with bayonets. If this failed to rejuvenate their interest in the march, they were shot. Many were physically unable to continue due to fatigue, disease, and hunger. Some simply lost the spirit to continue. Why Ben Steele was among those who never gave up is an imponderable, but perhaps the difficulties he had learned to face as a child on a Montana ranch during the drought years of the 1930s are a part of the explanation.

I have known only one other person who was an ex-prisoner of war, a captain in the German army who was taken prisoner by the Russians in the European Theater of World War II. Like Ben, he encountered cruel treatment at the hands of his captors, and like Ben he very nearly died of disease and starvation. However, he was a man marked by the experience. When one saw him walk down the street, one could tell that something dreadful and traumatic had happened in his past. His walk was always very brisk, and was interrupted frequently by a brief pause as he glanced over his shoulder to see who was behind him. When he ate, he gulped his food at an incredible rate. He was not a sociable person, but I remember one occasion when he began to reminisce about his home in Berlin before the war. An innocent question by someone present brought the story to an abrupt halt. Clearly, the memories were too painful and the feelings too bitter for him to continue.

I believe that art is central to the difference the prisoner of war experience had upon these two human beings. There were other differences. They came from vastly different backgrounds. And, after the war, one returned to his victorious homeland, while the other left his country to live in the land of the victors. The German probably did not receive psychiatric assistance in rehabilitating himself. Even so, both went on to pursue productive academic careers, and both even chose to adopt children into their families. Nonetheless, Ben Steele became a remarkably open, sharing, and sociable person. He is the one who seems unscarred by bitterness and resentment, and he is the one who made art both during and after the experience.

Sometimes artists resist talking about their art, saying "art is nonverbal." But nearly everything we talk about is nonverbal. Sensations, experiences and, especially, emotions are nonverbal. The first problem of communication is always to give these intangibles some sensible form that characterizes what is inside, outside ourselves. Until this is done, our thoughts and feelings, even our lives, mean nothing; we cannot fully comprehend what it is that has happened to us. When Ben first began drawing, he was battling boredom as well as disease. He was a burden to his fellow prisoners who had to secure provisions for him. When, through the drawings, he established his identity first as a Montanan, then as a recorder for the camp, his art gave form and meaning to existence and probably saved his life. That this function was important to the others is evidenced by their encouragement and direction. Others in the camp had died and were dying from any one of the five diseases that he was diagnosed as having simultaneously. Unlike those on the Bataan march who were shot because they were too exhausted and dispirited to go on, Ben got up from his sick bed and continued his march.

That unpleasant and frightful experiences are frequently repressed, becoming difficult or impossible to recall, is a fact well documented by psychological research. Experiences which have been acted upon and creatively given some form are seldom subject to such loss. During psychiatric treatment Ben could remember his lost drawings as discrete visual entities that helped trigger his recollections of the innumerable incidents locked in his subconscious. The re-created drawings are encapsulated personal experiences that he can re-experience and examine as though they were someone else's. They are objects. They are also encoded experiences, memories, and feelings, but they are no longer locked inside Ben's head. I believe that their existence as objects, made to be shared, is fundamental to Ben's open nature and lack of bitterness. They help give him perspective.

One of the drawings shows a Japanese guard pointing a bayonetted rifle at the belly of a captive. The captive, at the command of the guard, has just lifted his hat to reveal an onion balanced on top of his head. That soldier is Ben Steele, and the onion is one stolen from a truck garden that the captives were marched through on their way to forced labor in a Japanese coal mine. Ben witnessed the shootings of other prisoners for similar "crimes." He does not know why the guard did not kill him on the spot. We know that he has not forgotten that singular act of mercy by virtue of the drawing itself. I also know that he does not hate the Japanese people. In fact, one of the closest associations I ever saw him form with a student was with a young Japanese girl who came to the United States to complete her studies in art.

Ben's decision to study art came while he was still a prisoner of war. He was encouraged to continue his drawing by his psychiatrists who said it helped in the process of adjusting to civilian life. Once rehabilitated, he enrolled in and graduated from the Cleveland Institute of Art. Subsequently, he earned a BSE degree at Kent State and a MA degree at the University of Denver. He began his career as an artist/teacher in 1951. Very probably, he would not have become an artist were it not for the war. And, were it not for his growing up on a ranch in Montana, he might not have survived either the Bataan Death March or the subsequent imprisonment. Certainly his life means more to all of us because of his art.

A final thought is prompted by learning that Ben's prisoner of war camp on mainland Japan was less than eighty miles from Hiroshima where the first atom bomb was dropped. The bomb saved Ben Steele's life. The Japanese had told them that if the Allies invaded the mainland, all prisoners of war would be shot. That bomb was the first in a series of events that in a sense makes us all prisoners of war today. More than ever, we need to find those things in life that are meaningful and give them form; we need to have the perspective to take a long view that is free from bitterness; and we need to free ourselves of prejudice. In the face of a seemingly inevitable calamity, we need to find hope. I am glad Ben Steele survived and feel privileged to know him. He and his art have helped to shape my life.

1) The attack on Clark Field began at 12:25 p.m., December 8, 1941, Philippine time; the date in Hawaii was still December 7, (source: Hero of Bataan, Duane Schultz, St Martin's Press, NY, NY, 1981).

Benjamin Charles Steele
The Prisoner of War Drawings

by James Todd
Professor of Art and Humanities
University of Montana

War always weakens and often completely shatters the crust of customary decency which constitutes a civilization. It is a thin crust at the best of times, and beneath it...there is practically nothing of which human beings are not capable...

Aldous Huxley[1]

Little things that probably bother a lot of people don't bother me. I figure I'm probably living on a little borrowed time, and I'd better enjoy it.!

Ben Steele[2]

One of the most noteworthy aspects of Ben Steele's internment as a war prisoner and slave laborer of the Japanese during World War II was that these were the conditions by which he became an artist. The story of Steele's imprisonment possesses many remarkable aspects. It is remarkable that he survived the Bataan Death March and three-and-one-half years of slave labor in the Pacific War. It is also remarkable that it was under the constant threat of punishment and death that he executed this extensive series of drawings of prison life. Nonetheless, there remains the special uniqueness of a man finding and forming his vocation as a visual artist under these terrible circumstances. Many artists have given us powerful impressions of their reaction to war. Jean Callot, Goya, Otto Dix, and Picasso have expressed themselves concerning wars in their own times. Artists such as John Heartfield and George Grosz responded to conditions in their societies which threatened to create war. Maurice Lasansky in his "Nazi Drawings" and Maya Lin in her controversial Viet Nam War Memorial have responded to war after its occurrence. But Steele's drawings remain exceptional because he was a man lacking formal art training who used art as a means for personal survival and as a means to record the experiences of American war prisoners under Japanese Fascism.

The Prisoner of War drawings fall into three categories. The first includes the original drawings done in the prison camps. All but two of these were done between 1943 and 1944 in Bilibid Prison in the Philippines and were later lost at sea. The two original drawings which survive were done in 1945 on the Japanese mainland (pages 36 and 37). Fortunately, they give us an idea of the lost originals. The second category includes the drawings redone to replace the lost original drawings (pages 8-27). Steele did these between 1945 and 1947 during his post-war recuperation. When one compares the two extant originals with the 1945-47 drawings it is clear that the latter are very similar in execution and spirit to the originals. The third category of war drawings was created in 1952, after Steele had received formal art training. (pages 28-35)[3] These drawings were done in pen and ink, and they possess a superior technical proficiency and ease of gesture which is absent in the earlier drawings. However, they lack the concentrated detachment and seriousness of the unschooled drawings. The war drawings done before Steele went to art school possess an awkwardness, especially in respect to human anatomy. Yet the overall technical quality, consistency of feeling, and mastery of detail make it difficult to believe that the drawings were done by someone who had no professional art training and who had done practically no drawing at all in his life. The schooled drawings are stylistically reminiscent of the satirical cartoons of combat artists such as Bill Mauldin, and they possess a degree of caricature which tends to reduce their objectivity. By contrast, the earlier drawings make us aware that the artist was victim as well as reporter. In this respect they are spiritually akin to Aleksandr Solzhenitsyn's *One Day in the Life of Ivan Denisovich*. Steele's drawings share a direct and unpretentious realism with the Russian novel. Both Solzhenitsyn and Steele had a desperate need to give the public an accurate record of a secret and terrible legacy. Yet, Steele's drawings share something even more important with Solzhenitsyn's account of the Soviet Gulag. They are the record of a man who, through the healing power of art, transcended the conditions that were meant to degrade and dehumanize him.

Ben Steele was born in Roundup, Montana, in 1917. His parents were ranchers, and his father, Ben, Sr., came to Montana in 1890 from Canada by way of Missouri. His mother, Elizabeth, was a daughter of the McCleary family that opened the first coal mines in Roundup. Steele grew up on his parents' ranch twenty miles south of Musselshell, Montana. In 1932 the Great Depression brought his parents' ranching enterprise to an end. The young Ben Steele continued to work as a hand on ranches until he graduated from high school in 1939. Twice during his high school years he interrupted his studies to do ranch work. In 1940 he joined the Army Air Corps and eighteen months later he was a prisoner of the Japanese in the Philippines. Steele was captured in the fall of Bataan and participated in the notorious Bataan Death March, which was his introduction to the nightmare that life was to be for the next forty-two months as a prisoner of war.

The march was composed of approximately 8,000 American and 40,000 Philippine prisoners. At its end, some two weeks later, it is estimated that one quarter of the prisoners had died as a result of exhaustion, sickness, and execution by Japanese guards. As one of the March survivors, Steele worked as a slave laborer in the Tayabas road detail in southern Luzon. Steele claims that this work placed even greater demands on his capacity for survival than either the Death March or the last year of his imprisonment working in the coal mines on the Japanese mainland. Out of the original 325 men who worked with Steele in the Tayabas Road Detail, only fifty survived.

Later Steele became so ill from the combined effects of beri beri, dysentery, pneumonia, blood poisoning, and malaria that he was unable to work. He was placed in Bilibid Prison in Manila for eighteen months. It was during this period that he began to draw in an effort to maintain his sanity:

> I used to sit there day after day. I thought I'd lose my damn mind. I wanted something to do, so I started drawing with anything I could find to draw with. I'd draw on walls. People around me said, "Why don't you draw the guys? You know, there are no photographs taken of this stuff." So I started drawing stuff around the camp and sketches of people and portraits as close as I could. I wasn't very skillful.[4]

The decision to record his life as a prisoner was as dangerous for Steele as it was for artists imprisoned in Nazi concentration camps in Europe. The consequences of being caught making art could result in severe physical punishment, maiming, or death. It demanded great physical courage and concentrated will. Under these conditions Steele taught himself the fundamentals of perspective, anatomy, and composition while recording the everyday reality of prison life. He took charcoal from burnt ash, used the back sides of Japanese customs papers, and drew. Initially, he tried to do cowboy scenes from his Montana memories, but the experience of prison soon overwhelmed the Montana references, and he began to record the lives of Americans as prisoners of war, starting with the Bataan Death March.

By the end of his confinement in Bilibid Prison he had completed seventy drawings. Then in 1944 he and 1,100 other prisoners were shipped from Manila to Omine Machi, Japan, to work in coal mines. A Catholic priest named Father Duffy, a fellow prisoner who was chaplin for the Americans, had befriended Steele. Duffy knew about the drawings and agreed to hide them in his belongings while the prisoners were being shipped to the Japanese mainland. The ship upon which Duffy traveled was sunk, and Steele's drawings were lost. Miraculously, Duffy survived.

Following their arrival in Japan, Steele and the other prisoners were issued clothing for the first time in two years and were put to work in the coal mines at Omine Machi. The shifts lasted twelve hours, and there were no holidays except every tenth day when the prisoners were required to do other work such as carrying fertilizer. Steele claims that as difficult as this life was, it was an improvement over the disease-ridden work in the Philippine jungles. The regular work, however, made it impossible for Steele to continue his drawing, except for two drawings of life in the coal mines made shortly before his liberation.

The prison camp at Omine Machi was only seventy-five miles south of Hiroshima. Steele was a prisoner when the atomic bombs were dropped on that city and on Nagasaki. However, the prisoners were not aware of what had happened until after the war had ended. Steele recalls that on liberation American planes flew over and dropped large quantities of food to the prisoners. The danger of so much rich food for the emancipated camp inmates had not been understood. In some cases overeating caused inmates to become very ill.

Because of the severe deprivations he had endured, Steele was extremely weak and sick following his liberation. He spent a year after the war recuperating in a military hospital near Spokane, Washington. During that time he began to redraw the lost drawings from Bilibid Prison. His art again proved to be an important means by which he maintained his health and mental equilibrium. As Steele worked on these drawings, he was sensitive to his lack of formal training and decided to attend art school after his release from the hospital. He was admitted to the Cleveland Institute of Art on the strength of the war drawings and later attended Kent State University to complete his teaching credentials. In 1955 he earned a Masters Degree in art from the University of Denver.

It is now forty years since the end of World War II and the release of Ben Steele and the other Americans from the Japanese concentration camps. The current media nostalgia for the American past, including that war, has helped to bring long overdue attention to Steele's war drawings. At the end of the war, Americans were understandably reluctant to give attention to the war's bleaker side. For many, the important point was that the United States and its allies had won the war. This country was entering upon the most prosperous and influential period in its history. Ironically this included significant economic relations with post-war Japan. The defeats and humiliations had been overcome and were to be forgotten. Consequently, the Bataan Death March survivors were, in some respects, forgotten veterans. In a peculiar way, they suffered from public apathy similar to that experienced by the Viet Nam veterans of the current generation. Steele's war drawings, which depict Americans defeated and degraded at the hands of foreigners, were hardly the fare desired by a public flushed with victory.

The art world also was in no mood to give Steele's work much attention. During the late 1940's many artists and art critics were lauding the new American movements of Abstract Expressionism and non-objective painting. They tended to reject realist and narrative art as lacking in creativity and to praise the new abstract forms as truer and deeper expressions of American culture. In an article published in 1952, Harold Rosenberg, a major critic of the time and a supporter of the new painting movements, claimed:

> The big moment came when it was decided to paint....JUST TO PAINT....Liberation from the object meant liberation from the "nature," society and art already there. It was a movement to leave behind the self that wished to choose his future and to nullify its promissory notes to the past.[5]

Realism in art, especially that which expressed human conflict and collective concerns, was occasionally associated with the ideological art forms of Communism and Fascism, as well as with the WPA government-sponsored social realism of the 1930's. Many younger artists rejected traditional approaches and wanted something new and less social in content. In the rush to break from tradition, even craftsmanship was at times looked down upon. Steele remembers being told by an art professor that his (Steele's) "problem" was that he drew too well.

Time has altered these perspectives. We can now see clearly that the importance of Steele's drawings cannot be determined by the aesthetic debates of the 1940's and 1950's. Nor is their importance determined by the current romanticizing of combat and war. In Steele's work there is none of the muscle-inflated bravado that pervades the war stories of today's film and television programming. His drawings, like Goya's "Disasters of War," reveal the depravity of war itself. The Japanese in Steele's pictures are the tormentors because they carry guns, but the incarceration of Japanese-Americans during World War II and the American slaughter of defenseless civilians at Mai Li demonstrate that Americans are capable of their own war-inspired injustices and brutalities.

Ben Steele's contribution to humanity and art stemmed from his need to tell the truth despite its horror. In conditions of human torment and chaos, he expressed this truth with clarity and grace. His drawings were motivated by compassion for his fellow prisoners, and they are a means by which Steele achieved his own self-mastery. Theodore Adorno, the late German philosopher, is said to have asked how it is possible to write a poem after Auschwitz. Ben Steele's war drawings and his development as an artist and human being are the answer which tells us that not to do so is to forsake the struggle against barbarism and for human liberation.

---

[1]From a forward by Aldous Huxley to the *Complete Etchings of Goya*; Crown Publishing, New York, 1943.
[2]Quoted in "Ben Steele—Teacher," *EMC Update,* March, 1978; p. 3.
[3]The three paintings would also fit in the third category.
[4]Quoted in *Update* article.
[5]Harold Rosenberg, "The American Action Painters," *Art News,"* L1, *December, 1952, p. 23.*

The Bombing of Clark Field

The United States is not prepared for the Japanese attack on Pearl Harbor on December 7, 1941, or for the attack on Clark Field in the Philippines ten hours later on the same day. American troops on Luzon are bombed and strafed by approximately fifty bombers and one hundred fighter planes. They are not equipped for such an onslaught and are reduced to shooting at enemy planes with pistols

Philippine Scouts in Action

American-trained Philippine scouts engage the enemy in a small barrio during the Japanese drive toward Manila. These well-trained troops are excellent fighters.

Surprise Attack On The 26th Cavalry

A surprise attack by the Japanese involves the Philippine 26th
Horse Cavalry. Cavalry horses and other livestock are later
eaten on Bataan when food becomes scarce.

Capture

Many American and Philippine fighters are captured in small groups and individually before they reach the southern tip of Bataan at the mouth of Manila Bay. Two are forced to kneel along an ammunition trail while Japanese soldiers kick dirt on them, signing that they are "number one" and the kneelers low as dirt.

Beginning the March

After capture by the Japanese, 8,000 American and approximately 40,000 Philippine troops begin the march back up the Bataan Peninsula, staggering along the road for a period of ten days to two weeks. A Japanese wipes off his bayonet after killing a POW who has fallen out.

Death Marchers Drink From Mud Holes

With temperatures around 100 degrees, many men die from thirst. The Japanese have made no provisions to supply prisoners with water on the march. In desperation men lie on the ground to drink from a mud hole.

Eating Sugar Cane

When Japanese troops are not too close, captives on the Death March break ranks to go into the sugar cane fields to get cane to eat. If caught with the cane, a prisoner might be beaten or killed.

The Stragglers

Men unable to continue the march are killed by Japanese
guards. Fellow prisoners dare not intervene.

Hunger

The captives are only fed twice on the entire Death March. Philippine citizens throw cookies and biscuits from the side of the road and prisoners fight for them. Everyone is hungry.

Rules and Regulations

From the Death March prisoners go to Camp O'Donnell, a former Philippine Constabulary Camp. They are told, first by a Japanese officer and then by an interpreter, what they have to do to survive in the camp.

Chow Line at Camp O'Donnell

After cooking rice and seed potatoes in caldrons over wood fires, fellow prisoners bring them out in boxes at mealtime. Few POW's have mess equipment so they use their steel helmets or a piece of board or tin, anything to hold an issue of rice. Portions are small.

His Own

Approximately 2,300 Americans die and are buried at Camp O'Donnell the first six weeks of internment there. A soldier is forced to dig his own grave. Perhaps he tried to hit a Japanese guard or he possessed Japanese currency. He digs the grave and they bury him in it.

Water Brigade

Men carry canteens on poles and hollowed-out bamboo stalks
to and from the single water spigot at Camp O'Donnell. The
majority of prisoners are too ill to fight the water line.

Tayabas Road

With conditions so bad at Camp O'Donnell, prisoners volunteer for work details away from the camp. On the Tayabas Road detail, men walk 26 miles in from the railroad. The sick are carried in on doors to work. The road is built during the rainy season, July through August, with no shelter or blankets and 12-hour work shifts. Of the 325 men assigned to the project, only about 50 survive, making Tayabas Road the worst work detail in the Philippines.

Cooking Rice

Prisoners cook their own rice on the way to Tayabas Road. They use tin cans and canteen cups over open fires. At the work camp rice is cooked by the Japanese in wheelbarrows. Occasionally soup is served.

Tayabas Trenches

Straddle trenches are used as latrines on the detail. Some of the men are so ill from the effects of exposure to rain, hard work, dietary deficiency, and tropical diseases that they fall dead in the trenches. Lean-tos of nepa palm leaves form the only shelter.

Incentive to Work

The Japanese are hard taskmasters. Sick men are beaten for
not working fast enough to suit the guards.

Burial on Tayabas

Tayabas Road created countless "unknown soldiers." The dead are placed in individual graves with their dogtags tied to crossed sticks used as markers. Since the graves are on a flood plain, many bodies wash away or are covered by the jungle.

Tayabas Road Hospital

Prisoners too weak to make shelters for themselves lie on nepa leaves on the wet ground. Rain and Typhoons add to the misery. At the end of the two-month Tayabas Road detail only five or six "workers" can walk.

The Chapel At Bilibid

The men in Bilibid Prison build a crude chapel against one of the fortress walls for church services. All denominations worship here. By this time prisoners have taken the sleeves and legs off their clothing to patch what is left. They wear the same uniforms for two and a half years. They make "clackers" by nailing what remains of their shoes, the boot tops, to pieces of boards.

Quan And Quaning

As the prisoners understand it, the word "quan" means anything edible in the Philippine language. Eventually all prisoners obtain or make a can in which to collect and cook edible items (weeds, insects, snakes, etc.). The container becomes their "quan can," a very valuable possession.

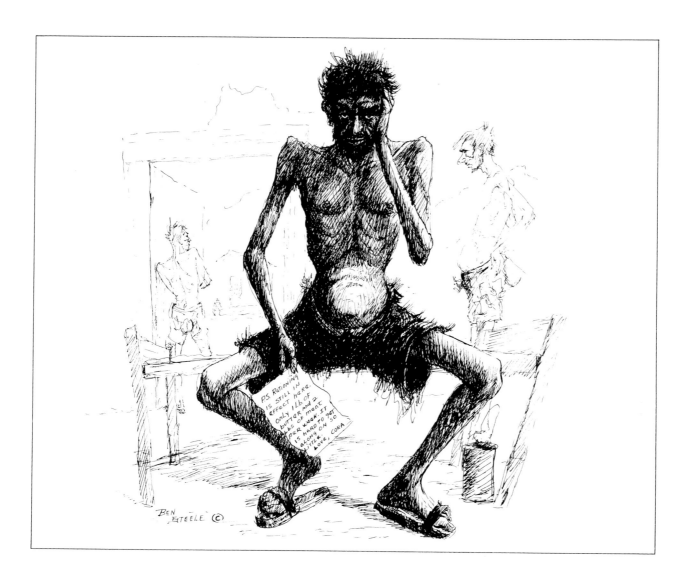

Letter From Home

The poor prisoner only wishes he had such troubles as related in the letter from home about rationing! Families and friends of prisoners have no conception of the conditions in the prison camps.

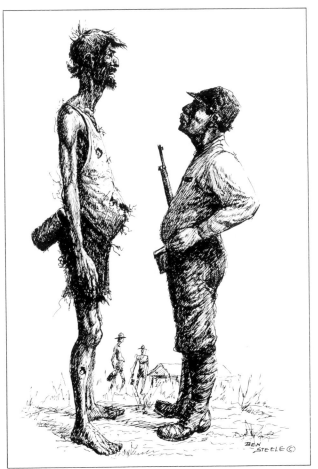 

Reprimanded and Shakedown

Workers on a farm try to conceal vegetables under their hats or clothing whenever possible. Every once in a while the Japanese stage a shakedown and those caught stealing the vegetables are beaten or put in solitary confinement.

Ready to Move

Old rice sacks are used to carry the few belongings of men about to move camp. Prisoners mend their clothing with pieces of wood, leather, and string. They make quan cans from pieces of tin and wire. These belongings become priceless.

Fair Game

Rats are fair game for quaning. Prisoners are issued very little
meat, fish, or other kinds of protein. The quest for meat is
constant.

Cabanatuan Beef

A prisoner gets his rat and is envied by a buddy. Few have the strength to catch a rat. The best time for hunting rats is at night when they come out to forage. Prisoners joke about their Cabanatuan "beef."

Chowline At Cabanatuan

Men line up to receive their rations of rice and soup. If they are lucky, there will be fishheads in the soup. Sometimes they are given green fish that is rotten. Once in a while the soup contains kelp.

Working The Mines

The Japanese practice drift mining of coal. Tunnels are supported or timbered as the coal is taken out. Prisoners taken to Japan to work in the coal mines are issued their first new clothing in two and a half years.

Warming Binto In Japan

"Binto" means lunch in Japanese. Water is boiled for barley husk tea, and soybean buns are warmed on a brazier. The buns are tasteless, hard, and nutritious. The brazier is heated with "sumi balls" made from slag coal. (This is one of the two surviving original drawings.)

Working Topside

Topside work at a Japanese coal mine is strenuous. The Japanese cut into a mountainside to make roadbeds for tracks. Prisoners load large rocks onto flatcars and then roll the cars to a fill and dump them. (This is the second of the two surviving original drawings.)

Chronology

November 17, 1917—Born Roundup, Montana

September 1923-June 1932—Attended grade school in Roundup and on family ranch south of Musselshell in the Bull Mountains.

September 1932—Moved from ranch to Billings, Montana.

June 1933—Graduated from eighth grade, Fratt Memorial School, Billings.

September 1933—Enrolled at Billings Senior High School.

June 1934—Left high school to work on Irving Harvey Ranch and Carroll Clark Ranch, Pompeys Pillar, Montana.

September 1935—Entered Huntley Project High School.

June 1936—Left high school to work at Clark Ranch, Pompeys Pillar and Big Hole Basin.

September 1937—Re-entered Senior High School.

June 1939—Graduated from Billings Senior High School.

June 1939-April 1940—Worked for Snook Art Company, Billings, as a glazier.

April 1940-September 1940—Worked for C.E. Clark, Hardin, Montana.

September 9, 1940—Enlisted in United States Army Air Corps at Fort Missoula.

September 1940—Arrived March Field, California for basic training.

April 1941—Ordered to Albuquerque, New Mexico and assigned to 7th Material Squadron, 19th Bombardment Group as aircraft dispatcher.

September 1941—Assigned to duty at Clark Field, Philippine Islands.

October 15, 1941—Arrived at Clark Field.

December 8, 1941—Clark Field attacked by Japanese.

December 25, 1941—Evacuated Clark Field; ordered to Bataan Peninsula.

January 6, 1942—Squadron assigned to infantry duty on front lines of Bataan.

April 7, 1942—Front lines collapsed.

April 9, 1942—Captured by Japanese near Cabcaben, Bataan.

April 10, 1942—Started "Death March of Bataan."

April 18, 1942—Arrived at Camp O'Donnell Prison Camp.

June 2, 1942—Assigned to Tayabas Road Detail.

August 15, 1942—Taken to Bilibid Prison, Manila, from Tayabas Road—too ill to work; began to draw.

January 1944—Sent to Cabanatuan Prison Camp.

July 2, 1944—Returned to Bilibid Prison.

July 4, 1944—Loaded aboard freighter "Canadian Inventor," named "Mati Mati Maru" by prisoners.

September 2, 1944—Landed Moji, Japan.

September 3, 1944—Arrived Omine Machi Coal Mine, Japan

August 6, 1945—Heard atom bomb dropped on Hiroshima.

August 15, 1945—Work ceased in coal mines.

August 18, 1945—American planes dropped food, clothing, medical supplies, and leaflets into camp.

September 10, 1945—Boarded train and met occupation troops at Wakayama, Japan.

September 12, 1945—Left Wakayama on "U.S.S. Constellation" hospital ship.

September 16, 1945—Arrived Okinawa.

September 18, 1945—Flown by 19th Bombardment Group C54 to Guam via Iwo Jima.

September 24, 1945—Arrived Hickam Field, Hawaii.

September 26, 1945—Landed in San Francisco; taken to Letterman General Hospital.

October 10, 1945—Assigned to Baxter General Hospital, Spokane, Washington.

November 15, 1945—Went home to Billings for first time in over five years.

December 1, 1945—Assigned to Fort George Wright Hospital, Spokane, Washington.

February 16, 1946—Married Roberta Mellis in Billings.

July 10, 1946—Discharged from United States Air Force.

December 12, 1946—Daughter Rose Marie born in Portland, Oregon.

September 1947—Enrolled in Cleveland Institute of Art.

November 3, 1947—Daughter Julie Margaret born in New London, Ohio.

September 1949—Divorced from Roberta Mellis.

June 1950—Graduated from Cleveland Institute of Art; enrolled in Kent State University.

June 1951—Graduated from Kent State University with B.S.E. Degree.

June 1951—Began summer school at Denver University.

September 1951—Taught art and coached at New London (Ohio) High School, 1951-52 school year.

August 31, 1952—Married Shirley Ann Emerson at New London, Ohio.

March 1953—Employed by Department of Army as Post Crafts Director, Fort Riley, Kansas.

December 1954—Appointed Staff Crafts Director, Military District of Washington, Washington, D.C.

June 1955—Awarded M.A. Degree from Denver University.

June 1956—Appointed Staff Crafts Director, Third United States Army, Fort MacPherson, Georgia.

September 1959—Began teaching in Art Department, Eastern Montana College, Billings, Montana.

September 1965—Appointed Director of Art Department.

March 1966—Adopted son Sean Emerson.

September 1970—Appointed Head of Art Department.

June 1982—Retired as Professor of Art Emeritus, Eastern Montana College.

List of Works in the Exhibit

Drawings

1. The Bombing of Clark Field
   21 1/4" x 28"
2. Phillipine Scouts in Action
   21" x 28"
3. Surprise Attack on 26th Cavalry
   17 1/2" x 28"
4. Japanese Attack
   18 3/4" x 28"
5. Constabulary Troops Engage Japanese
   15 1/2" x 28"
6. Battle for Guagua
   15" x 18"
7. High Command—General Wainwright
   16 1/4" x 23"
8. Capture
   11" x 14"
9. Beginning the March
   11 1/2" x 18 3/4"
10. Drinking From Mud Hole—Death March
    11 1/2" x 12 1/2"
11. Degradation—Death March
    10" x 14 1/2"
12. Breaking Ranks—Death March
    14" x 29 1/4"
13. Helping a Buddy #1—Death March
    11" x 17"
14. Taking Shoes Off a Dead POW—Death March
    9" x 11 1/2"
15. Exhausted POW—Death March
    11 3/4" x 18 1/4"
16. Falling Out of Ranks—Death March
    22 1/2" x 27 1/4"
17. Getting Water—Death March
    19 1/4" x 24"

18. Eating Sugar Cane—Death March
    16 1/4" x 23"
19. Helping a Friend #2—Death March
    11 3/4" x 17 1/4"
20. Kicking an Exhausted POW—Death March
    11 1/2" x 18 1/2"
21. Shooting a Straggler—Death March
    9" x 12"
22. Bayoneting a Straggler—Death March
    9" x 12"
23. Beating a Straggler—Death March
    11" x 17"
24. The Fallouts—Death March
    9" x 15 1/2"
25. Hunger—Death March
    11" x 17"
26. San Fernando Enclosure—Death March
    11 1/2" x 18 1/2"
27. Rules & Regulations—Camp O'Donnell
    19 1/4" x 27 1/4"
28. Prisoner of War—Camp O'Donnell
    7 1/2" x 8"
29. Chow Line at Camp O'Donnell
    9 1/4" x 11 1/2"
30. Filipinos Carrying Their Dead—Camp O'Donnell
    7 1/2" x 10"
31. Helping a Friend #3—Camp O'Donnell
    8 3/4" x 18"
32. His Own—Camp O'Donnell
    18 3/4" x 27 1/2"

33. Dysentery River
    8 1/2" x 11 1/2"
34. Precious Water—Camp O'Donnell
    7 3/4" x 11"
35. Buried Alive—Camp O'Donnell
    14 3/4" x 25 3/4"
36. Water Brigade—Camp O'Donnell
    20 1/4" x 27 1/2"
37-38. Prayer-Wounded—Camp O'Donnell
    9 1/2" x 8"   9 1/2" x 8"
39. March to Tayabas—Tayabas Road
    8 1/2" x 11 1/2"
40. Cooking Rice—Tayabas Road
    11" x 18"
41. The Beggars—Tayabas Road
    11" x 9"
42. Arrival at Tayabas—Tayabas Road
    16 1/2" x 22"
43. A Beating—Tayabas Road
    8 1/2" x 11"
44. Dysentery Area—Tayabas Road
    7 3/4" x 11 1/4"
45. Incentive to Work—Tayabas Road
    7 1/2" x 10"
46. Burial on Tayabas Road
    8" x 11 1/4"
47. Going to Work—Tayabas Road
    11 1/4" x 18 1/2"
48. Coming in From Work—Tayabas Road
    7 1/2" x 10 1/4"
49. Carrying Items for Japanese—Tayabas Road
    9" x 15 1/2"
50. Tayabas Road Hospital
    9" x 11 1/2"

51. Camp Area—Tayabas Road
9" x 11 1/2"

52. Tayabas Detail Arrival—Bilibid
8 1/2" x 11 1/2"

53. Chow Line—Bilibid
10 1/2" x 12 3/4"

54. The Chapel at Bilibid
8 3/4" x 11"

55. Ward #11—Bilibid
8 1/2" x 10"

56. Taking Pig's Food—Bilibid
7 1/2" x 11"

57. Old Man—Bilibid
9" x 13"

58. Quan and Quaning—Bilibid
11" x 13 1/4"

59. Changing Camps—Cabanatuan
8 3/4" x 11"

60. Lucky Man—Bilibid
11 1/2" x 14"

61. Letter From Home—Bilibid
8 1/2" x 9 1/4"

62. Fenced In—Cabanatuan
10 1/2" x 9"

63. Nichols Field—Nichols Field
11 1/2" x 14"

64-65. Reprimanded-Shakedown—Cabanatuan
12" x 7 1/2"   8" x 11 1/2"

66. Carrying Vegetables—Cabanatuan
8 1/2" x 13"

67. Ready to Move—Cabanatuan
11 1/2" x 14 1/2"

68. Quanning #2—Cabanatuan
12" x 14 1/4"

69. Beating a POW—Nichols Field
9" x 13"

70. Honey Bucket Detail—Philippines
10 1/4" x 14"

71. Changing Camps—Cabanatuan
10 1/4" x 13 1/2"

72. Fair Game—Cabanatuan
8 1/2" x 12 1/2"

73. Cabanatuan Beef—Cabanatuan
10 1/2" x 11"

74. Disagreement—Cabanatuan
11 1/2" x 14"

75. Chow Line at Cabanatuan
11" x 12"

76. Working in Coal Mines—Omine Machi, Japan
10 1/2" x 13 3/4"

77. Beating a POW—Omine Machi, Japan
9" x 10 1/2"

78. Working the Mines—Omine Machi, Japan
10 1/2" x 27 1/2"

79. Rousting a Sleeper—Omine Machi, Japan
9 1/4" x 12 1/2"

80. Warming Binto in Japan—Omine Machi, Japan
7" x 9 1/2"

81. Working Topside—Omine Machi, Japan
6 3/4" x 9 1/4"

Paintings

1. Waterline—Camp O'Donnell   Oil on Hardboard
24" x 48"

2. The Beggars—Tayabas Road   Oil on Canvas
24" x 32"

3. Rice and Men—Tayabas Road   Oil on Canvas
30" x 38"

The Ben Steele Prisoner of War Collection has been exhibited at:

Baxter Hotel, Spokane, Washington, 1945.

Baumgartner Studio, Billings, Montana, 1946.

Miami, Florida, 1946.

Cleveland Institute of Art, 1948.

Kent State University, 1950.

Counter Intelligence Corps, New York City, 1951.

Fifth United States Army Area, 1953.

Little Gallery By The Sea, The Dalles, Oregon, 1953.

Third United States Army Area, 1957.

Georgia Institute of Technology, Atlanta, Georgia, 1958.

Eastern Montana College, Billings, Montana, 1960.

DeMolay Gallery, Great Falls, Montana, 1961.

Big Horn County Court House, Hardin, Montana 1963.

Eastern Montana College, 1963.

Butte, Montana, 1964.

College of Great Falls, Great Falls, Montana, 1966.

Muehlbach Hotel, ADBC, Kansas City, Missouri, 1973.

Copper Village Museum and Art Center, Anaconda, Montana, 1973.

Ketterer Art Center, Bozeman, Montana, 1974.

Montana Historical Society Museum, Helena, Montana, 1974.

Yellowstone Art Center, Billings, Montana, 1974.

Montana Institute of the Arts Festival, Dawson County High School, Glendive, Montana, 1976.

Gillette High School, Gillette, Wyoming, 1977.

Scottsdale Center for the Arts, Scottsdale, Arizona, 1978.

C.M. Russell Museum, Great Falls, Montana, 1978.

Liberal Arts Gallery, Eastern Montana College, 1981.

Musselshell Valley Historical Museum, Roundup, Montana, 1983.

They have appeared on television in Washington, D.C.; Atlanta, Georgia; Billings, Montana; and nationally on ABC's *20/20*.